Claude

The True Story of a White Alligator

Emma Bland Smith   Illustrated by **Jennifer M. Potter**

Story written with permission of the California Academy of Sciences

little bigfoot

an imprint of sasquatch books
seattle, wa

In a Louisiana swamp, a baby alligator cracked out of his shell.

Like his many sisters and brothers, he was about the size of a banana. Like them, he had a long tail and scaly skin. Like them, he was quite cute.

But unlike his siblings, this little alligator was *not green*. He was white.

This was an *albino* alligator.

He was different from the other alligators. Very different. And in the swamp, *different* can be dangerous.

He didn't blend in with his surroundings, so he couldn't hide from hungry herons or raccoons.

His pink eyes didn't see well, so when he got older, it would be hard for him to find food.

And his pale skin could get badly burned in the hot southern sun.

Worst of all, his differentness made the other alligators uneasy.

The baby alligator was in danger.

The man who ran the alligator farm was worried. *This little guy needs protection*, he thought. So he gave him to a special zoo in Florida that raised and cared for alligators and other animals.

The zookeepers named him Claude. To protect him,
they put him in a pen by himself.

He was safe now, but all alone.

Claude lived alone for almost thirteen years. Until one day, biologists at a museum in faraway California heard about him.

They were excited. A white alligator? How different! How wonderful!

They wanted Claude to come to their museum. And they had the perfect place for him to live.

The biologists also asked the zoo for a second alligator. Claude had been alone all his life. They hoped that in this new home things could be different. Maybe the other alligator, Bonnie, would accept Claude. Maybe they'd even become friends.

So Claude—who was by then eight feet long—took an almost 2,800-mile, four-day road trip. A professional wild-animal handler drove both alligators all the way across the United States to the California Academy of Sciences in San Francisco.

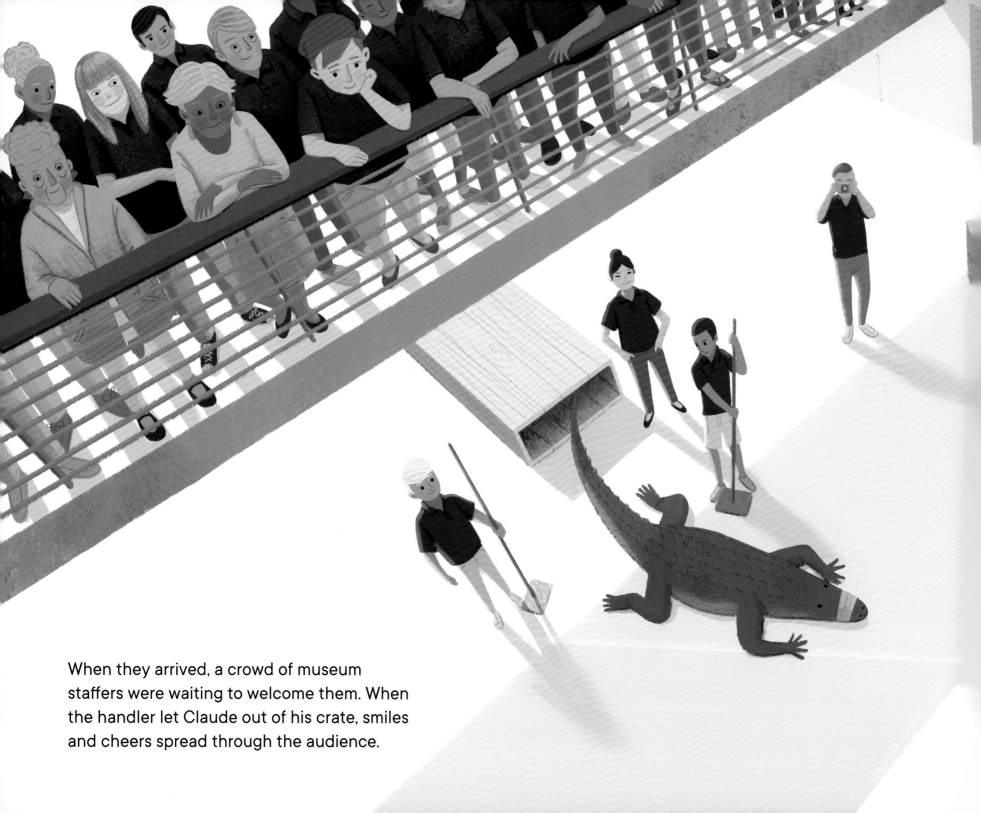

When they arrived, a crowd of museum staffers were waiting to welcome them. When the handler let Claude out of his crate, smiles and cheers spread through the audience.

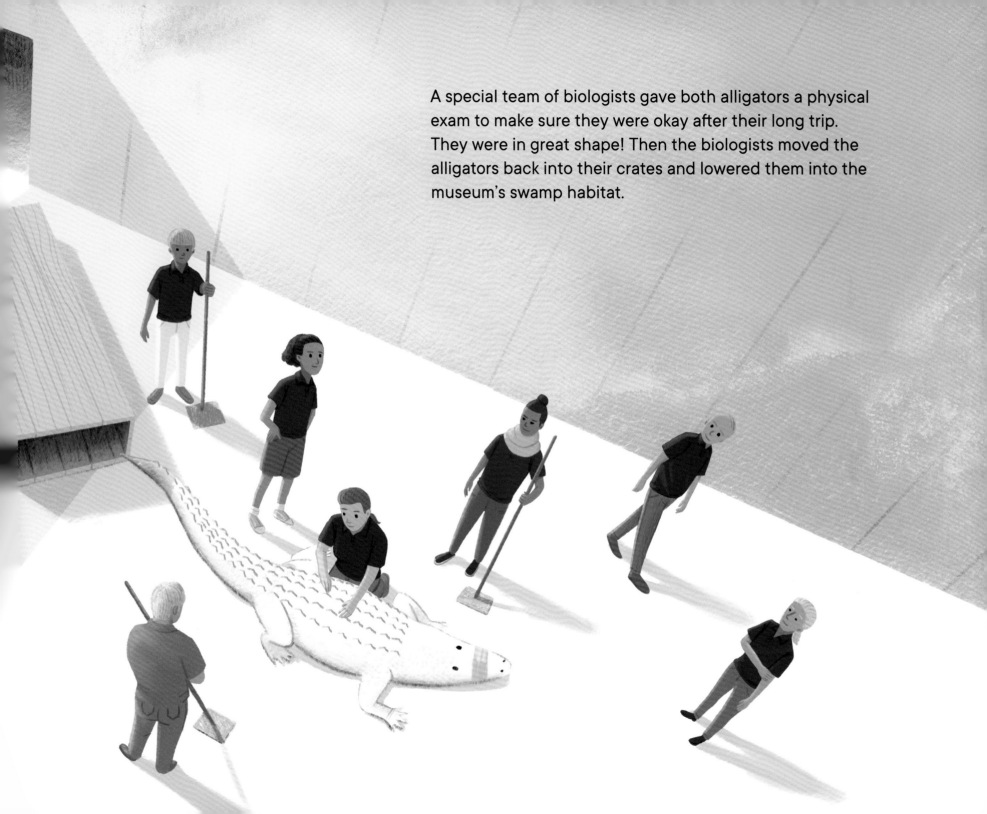

A special team of biologists gave both alligators a physical exam to make sure they were okay after their long trip. They were in great shape! Then the biologists moved the alligators back into their crates and lowered them into the museum's swamp habitat.

The crowd watched anxiously. Would Claude like his new home? Would he and Bonnie get along?

Claude explored his new swamp. It was warm. It had plants. And trees. And a fancy heated island!

Over the next few months, Bonnie and Claude shared
their swamp. They swam together. They ate together.
They even shared the heated island.

But Bonnie didn't like Claude. She didn't like how he bumped into things because of his bad eyesight. She didn't like how he bumped into *her*.

So one day she bit him on the foot. Hard.

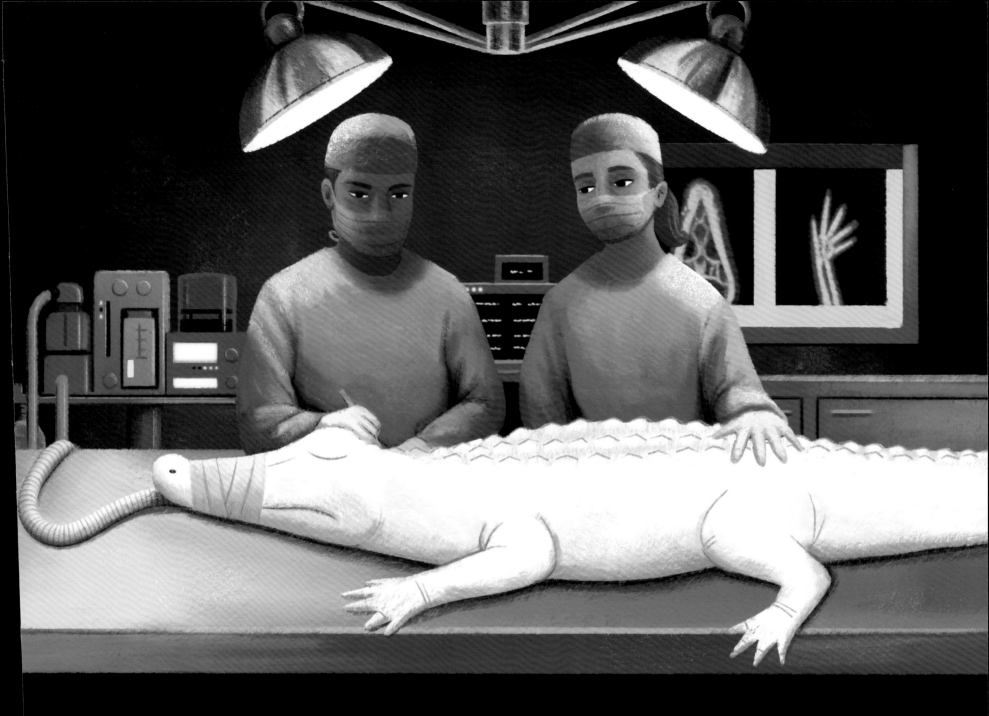

Poor Claude! The biologists hoisted him out of the swamp. Then they
operated on him to remove his pinkie toe. Claude took two weeks to recover.

When he returned to the swamp, Bonnie was gone.
The biologists had sent her back to Florida.

Once again, Claude was all alone.

Or was he?

In all the stress of sharing the swamp with Bonnie, Claude had hardly noticed his other swamp mates, five enormous snapping turtles. Leonardo, Donatello, Raphael, Morla, and Jaws were rescue animals too. They had been saved from the illegal turtle trade forty years before Claude arrived in San Francisco.

Would they attack Claude? Would he attack them?

What happened next was a surprise.

They became friends.

After all, they enjoyed the same things,

like good food,

a new toy,

Turtle being
cleaned by fish

Claude getting his monthly
shower and massage

and bath time.

Sometimes they squabbled, as friends do. Once, Leonardo decided to check out Claude's fancy heated island. Claude was annoyed. He sat on Leonardo.

But eventually, they worked it out.

The turtles didn't mind that Claude was different from other alligators. (They were turtles, for goodness' sake!) For the first time in his life, Claude had buddies.

Claude made other friends as well. People from all around the world came to San Francisco to meet him. *A white alligator? How different! How wonderful!* they thought.

His fans drew pictures of him
and wrote him letters.

They bought stuffed white
alligators at the museum shop
to take home and cuddle.

And on his "hatchday," they
threw him a huge party!

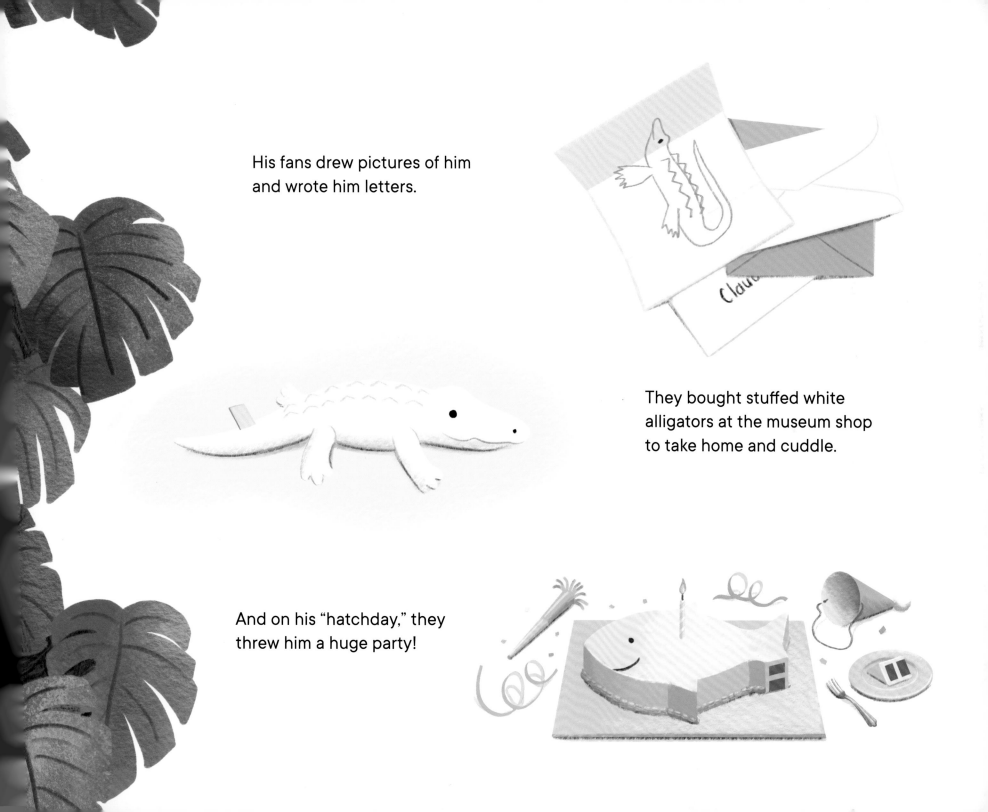

Claude was a celebrity!

He was also an ambassador for science. Visitors learned about how habitat destruction is hurting wildlife. They learned about camouflage and animal behavior and the genetic code that makes each creature unique—including Claude. They learned that there are hardly any albino alligators in the whole world—probably fewer than thirty!

Claude was no longer alone. Now he had friends by the thousands! The lonely, outcast alligator had become the most loved alligator in the world.

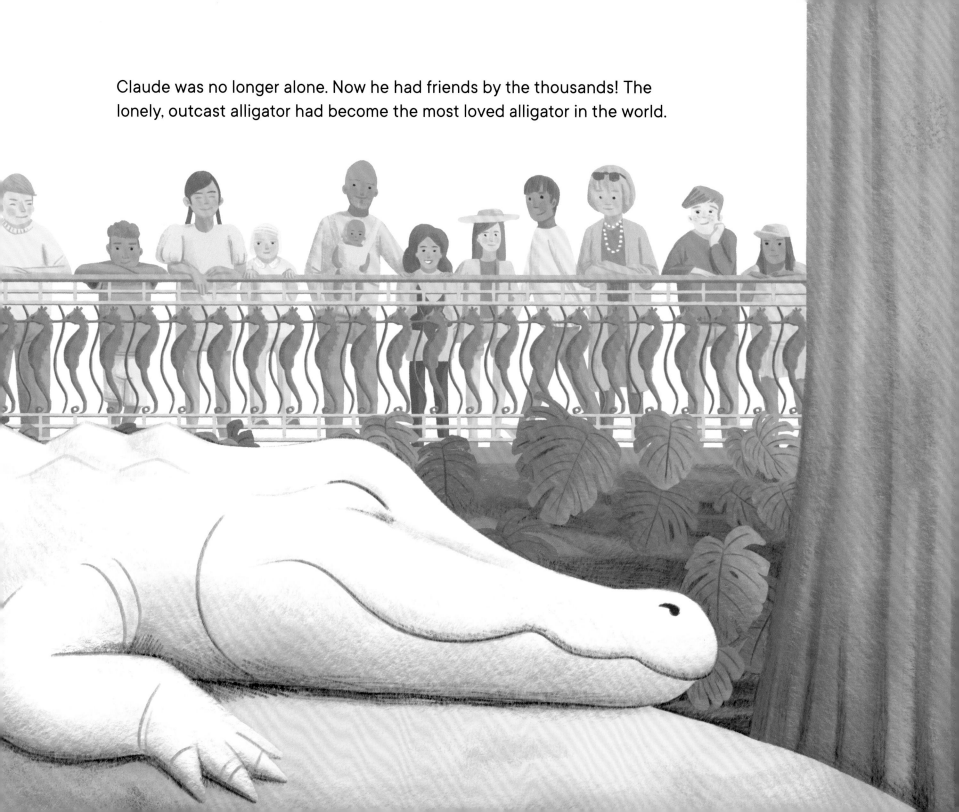

Claude was still different. Very different. But in *this* swamp, *different* was wonderful.

COMMON QUESTIONS ABOUT CLAUDE

Where is Claude from?

Claude was hatched on an alligator farm in Louisiana in 1995. Within twenty-four hours, he was relocated to the St. Augustine Alligator Farm Zoological Park in Florida. Claude lived there until 2008, when he moved to the California Academy of Sciences, along with his short-term swamp mate, Bonnie.

What is the difference between alligators and crocodiles?

Alligators are native only to two places: the southeastern United States and China. Crocodiles, on the other hand, are found in Asia, Africa, Australia, and the Americas. Alligators are smaller and less aggressive (they rarely attack humans). If you look closely, you can easily tell them apart: alligators' snouts are more rounded, and only crocodiles have bottom teeth that show when their mouth is closed.

Why is Claude white?

Claude was born with a condition called albinism, which can also affect people and other animals. Albinism is caused by the body's inability to produce a substance called melanin, which gives color to our hair, skin, and eyes. This is why Claude has yellowish-white skin and pinkish eyes. Like many features, albinism is passed down from parents to offspring by genes—microscopic markers that provide instructions to our bodies—that make us who we are. Like Claude, people with albinism are very vulnerable to sun damage and often have impaired vision. But just like Claude, they know that different can be wonderful.

How many albino alligators are there?

Experts believe that none exist in the wild, and that in human care, there are probably fewer than thirty.

Why can't albino alligators live in the wild?

Their white skin makes them stand out. As a baby, Claude would have been snatched up and eaten almost instantly by a raccoon, otter, bobcat, bird, or even another alligator. If he did somehow make it to adulthood in the wild, he would have had trouble sneaking up on prey.

Why did Bonnie bite Claude?

Biologists at the California Academy of Sciences hoped that in a controlled environment, the two alligators would be able to overlook their differences. Bonnie had even been "personality tested" back in Florida to live with Claude. Unfortunately, Bonnie was unsettled by the clumsiness Claude's impaired vision caused. She picked on Claude, until she eventually injured his toe. Bonnie was returned to the St. Augustine Alligator Farm in Florida and lives there still.

Where did the snapping turtles come from?

Over forty years ago, five female alligator snapping turtles were confiscated in San Francisco's Chinatown, where they were on their way to becoming someone's turtle-soup dinner. They have been living in the swamp habitat of the California Academy of Sciences ever since. Sadly, in 2019 Leonardo, one of the five turtles, passed away. The remaining turtles weigh between 50 and 125 pounds each.

How do biologists train Claude?

They use positive reinforcement, particularly food rewards, like you would use to train a dog. Claude also quickly learned to respond to a clicker, whistles, and even words. Contrary to popular belief, alligators are very intelligent animals.

What does Claude eat?

He eats fish, rodents, chicken, and a special gator chow.

How long will Claude live?

Alligators in human care can reach the age of eighty. Claude was born in 1995. He may live at the California Academy of Sciences until the year 2075!

How big is Claude?

Today he is about ten feet long and weighs around 275 pounds. And he's still growing!

How long have there been alligators at the California Academy of Sciences?

The Academy's world-famous Steinhart Aquarium, located in San Francisco's Golden Gate Park, has had alligators since 1923. The alligator habitat was completely rebuilt during the museum's major renovation that ended in 2008, but the iconic seahorse railing and painted tiles were retained. Today, Claude the alligator serves as a charismatic ambassador for his species, delighting and educating over a million visitors each year.

Many thanks to all the staff at the California Academy of Sciences for their help and support, and to John Brueggen and everyone at the St. Augustine Alligator Farm Zoological Park, who cared for Claude during the first thirteen years of his life. —EBS

For my mom, Sally Bland, the Academy's most faithful member —EBS

For my dad, Jon Potter, who's a bit different and wonderful himself —JMP

Claude enjoying his heated island at the California Academy of Sciences

Manufactured in China by C&C Offset Printing Co. Ltd. Shenzhen, Guangdong Province, in March 2020

LITTLE BIGFOOT with colophon is a registered trademark of Penguin Random House LLC

24 23 22 21 20   9 8 7 6 5 4 3 2 1

Editors: Christy Cox, Michelle McCann
Production editor: Bridget Sweet
Designer: Anna Goldstein
Photograph of Claude: *Claude on Rock*, Image No. 0639 by Kathryn Whitney, © 2014 California Academy of Sciences

Library of Congress Cataloging-in-Publication Data
Names: Smith, Emma Bland, author. | Potter, Jennifer M. (Jennifer Michelle), illustrator.
Title: Claude : the true story of a white alligator / Emma Bland Smith ; illustrated by Jennifer M. Potter.
Description: Seattle, WA : Little Bigfoot, [2020] | Audience: Ages 4–8. | Audience: Grades K–1.
Identifiers: LCCN 2019052977 | ISBN 9781632172693 (hardcover)
Subjects: LCSH: Alligators–Juvenile literature. | Alligators–Color–Genetic aspects–Juvenile literature. | Albinos and albinism–Juvenile literature. | Zoo animals–Juvenile literature.
Classification: LCC SF408.6.A54 S65 2020 | DDC 597.98/4147–dc23
LC record available at https://lccn.loc.gov/2019052977

ISBN: 978-1-63217-269-3

Sasquatch Book
1904 Third Avenue, Suite 710
Seattle, WA 98101

SasquatchBooks.com